American Lives

Dolores Huerta

Jennifer Blizin Gillis

Heinemann Library
Chicago, Illinois

Designed by Q2A Creative

Printed in China by WKT Limited

10 09 08 07 06
10 9 8 7 6 5 4 3 2 1

Library of Congress Cataloging-in-Publication Data
Gillis, Jennifer Blizin, 1950-
   Dolores Huerta / Jennifer Blizin Gillis.
      p. cm. – (American lives)
   Includes bibliographical references and index.
   ISBN 1-4034-6980-6 (hc) – ISBN 1-4034-6987-3
      (pb)
   1. Huerta, Dolores, 1930—Juvenile literature.
2. Women labor leaders–United States–Biography–
Juvenile literature. 3. Mexican American women labor union members–United States–Biography–
Juvenile literature. 4. Mexican American migrant agricultural laborers–Labor unions–Organizing–
United States–History–Juvenile literature.
5. Migrant agricultural laborers–Labor unions–
United States–History–Juvenile literature. I. Title.
II. Series: American lives (Heinemann Library
(Firm))
HD6509.H84G55 2006
331.4'7813'092–dc22
                       2005010127

Acknowledgments
The author and publishers are grateful to the following for permission to reproduce copyright material:

AP/Wide World Photos pp. 6, 12, 23, 27, 28; AP/Wide World Photos p. 24 (Jack Plunkett); Archives of Labor & Urban Affairs, Wayne State University pp. 4, 21; Corbis pp. 5 (Ted Streshinsky), 8 (Dorthea Lange); Corbis/Bettmann pp. 25 (Jeff Franko), 11, 13, 18, 22; Corbis/Bettmann/UPI p. 19; Corbis/National Archives p. 14; Corbis/San Francisco Chronicle p. 29 (Scott Sommerdorf); Getty Images/Time Life Pictures pp. 7 (Dmitri Kessel), 10 (Allan Grant), 15 (Arthur Schatz); Getty Images/Topical Press Agency p. 9; Take Stock pp. 16, 17, 20 (George Ballis), 26 (Bob Fitch).

Cover photograph of Dolores Huerta reproduced with permission of The Image Works/ Mark Ludak.

Every effort has been made to contact copyright holders of any material reproduced in this book. Any omissions will be rectified in subsequent printings if notice is given to the publisher.

Some words are shown in bold, **like this**. You can find out what they mean by looking in the glossary.

Contents

Strike!

In 1965, Dolores Huerta was at a meeting of the National Farm Workers Association (NFWA) in Delano, California. It was a **union** she and her friend César Chávez had started three years before. It was still very small, because it was against the law for farm workers to form unions.

California grape growers paid their workers almost nothing and made them work in terrible conditions. Another farm workers' union had asked Dolores and César's union to join their **strike** against the growers.

Dolores Huerta (in the white shirt on the right) went from field to field, telling workers to stand up for their rights.

Strikers ask others to join the strike. They hoped the strike would get them better pay and working conditions.

All of the workers were afraid of losing their jobs if they joined the strike. Dolores and César were worried, too. The growers were powerful people. But if the unions did not work together, the growers would never stop mistreating their workers.

The union members held a vote. They wanted to join the strike! Dolores did not know then that it would last for five years. But she believed that the farm workers had the power to change their lives. From then on, whenever she heard a tired worker say, "It can't be done," Dolores replied, *"Sí, se puede."* "Yes, it can be done."

Childhood

Dolores Fernandez Huerta was born in Dawson, New Mexico on April 10, 1930. Her father, Juan Fernandez, was a miner and an **activist.** He helped workers try to get better working conditions.

These workers in the 1930s had to travel around to find crops to pick.

In those days, many people could not find full-time jobs. Dolores sometimes traveled with her parents and her two siblings to find part-time work picking crops.

Timeline

1930	1955	1962	1965
Dolores is born on April 10	*Goes to work for the CSO*	*Starts National Farm Workers Association (NFWA) with César Chávez*	*Joins the "Great Grape **Strike**"*

Dolores was about six years old when her parents divorced. Her mother, Alicia Chávez, took Dolores and her siblings to Stockton, California. She got a job as a waitress in a restaurant. She also worked in a factory, canning food.

There is a lot of farm land around Stockton, California.

1966	1973	1988	1998	1999
Gets **contract** with Schenley Industries to pay workers fairly	Helps organize second **boycott** of California grapes	Beaten and badly injured by police	Chosen as a "Woman of the Year"	Receives award from President Bill Clinton

Growing Up

Dolores's mother married a man named James Richards. They bought a small hotel. Dolores and her siblings worked there after school.

The people who stayed at the hotel were **migrant** farm workers. They made very little money. Sometimes they could not pay their rent, but Dolores's mother did not make them leave. She made sure they had food to eat, too.

Migrant workers often lived in tiny shacks like this one.

Preparing fruit for canning was a hard and dangerous job because workers used very sharp knives, and the fruit was slippery.

Dolores felt at home in her neighborhood. No one looked down on her because she was a **Latina.** She liked school and often wrote stories and poems. She took music and dancing lessons and joined the Girl Scouts.

Some summers Dolores worked in a fruit canning factory. She sliced open apricots and put them on trays. She earned money for each tray she filled with fruit. It took all day to fill just a few trays!

High School and Marriage

Things changed when Dolores went to high school. One teacher would not give her a good grade on a paper she wrote. The teacher said Dolores must have cheated. She believed that **Latinos** could not write well.

Another time, Dolores organized a club for teenagers. They could go there to listen to music, dance, and play games. When the police found out that African-American, Latino, and white students went there together, they closed down the club.

Schools where children of different races studied together (such as this one) were once rare in parts of the United States.

In the 1950s most young women married soon after high school. Then, they were expected to stay home and keep the house clean.

After Dolores finished high school, she decided to go to college. That was very unusual in those days.

Dolores left college to marry. She and her husband had two daughters named Lori and Celeste. She had goals other than being a housewife. Her marriage did not last. She and her daughters moved in with Alicia. Dolores went back to college to become a teacher.

Teacher and Helper

Migrant workers often had to live in tents or shacks that had no toilets or running water.

Dolores was in her mid-twenties when she became a school teacher. Most of the students were children of **migrant** farm workers. Many of them had clothes or shoes that were falling apart. Often, they were so hungry that they could not pay attention in class.

Dolores wanted to do something to help their families. She heard about a group called the Community Service Organization, or CSO. It helped migrant workers get better working and living conditions.

Migrant Workers

*Migrant workers are often **Latinos**. Sometimes they live and work in very bad conditions. They earn very little money. Because many do not speak English, it is hard for them to get other jobs.*

Dolores knew that women in migrant families did the same hard work as the men, but they were paid less. At the end of the workday, they still had to prepare food and take care of their families. She began to speak up for women's rights, too.

In 1955 Dolores left her teaching job to start a CSO group in Stockton, California. Her friends thought she was crazy to agree to work for no money!

Fred Ross, the man on the left, talking to César Chávez, persuaded Dolores to volunteer with the CSO.

Speaking Out

One big problem for **migrant** workers was a law that had allowed farmers to bring in workers from Mexico during **World War II**. This law also said that farm workers could not form **unions**.

The war was over, but the law had not been changed. If migrant workers organized in groups or asked for more money or better working conditions, farmers fired them. Then, they brought in workers from Mexico. The farmers paid those workers far less than they paid the migrant workers.

After World War II, farmers kept bringing in workers from Mexico.

Dolores met with lawmakers to help migrant workers. She carried her papers in a grape box.

Some migrant farm workers were **citizens** of the United States, but they had never voted. Dolores helped them register to vote so they could elect lawmakers who would help them.

Farm owners sometimes cheated workers who could not read or write. Dolores organized night classes for English, reading, and writing.

Dolores started the Agricultural Workers Association. This group worked to get new laws passed. These laws helped migrant workers who got sick or hurt on the job get food and money. Dolores worked to end the law that allowed farmers to hire workers from Mexico.

A Soldier's Life

This is a picture of Dolores and her children singing with members of the NFWA in 1966.

Dolores married a man named Ventura Huerta and had five more children. They grew up going to meetings and **strikes**. They helped by holding signs or handing out papers about the farm workers' problems.

Her friends said that Dolores was like a woman soldier. She worked long hours. She traveled all over California. Ventura was not happy that Dolores was so involved with her work. Finally, they divorced.

Part of Dolores's job was to get workers to form small groups. Then, she tried to get big **unions** to let the small groups join them. The big unions often ignored the small groups of workers that joined. As time went by, Dolores began to think things would never get better for **migrant** workers. Farmers were still cheating and mistreating them. The workers needed some other way for their voices to be heard.

Union speakers went into **taverns** and pool halls to talk to as many workers as they could.

Meeting César

When Dolores started working with the Community Service Organization (CSO) in the 1950s, she met a man named César Chávez. He had been working for the CSO for about ten years. In 1959, he became president of the CSO.

Dolores and César shared many of the same ideas about workers' rights. In 1962, César decided that the workers must start their own union. But the CSO voted not to allow this. César left the CSO and moved his family to Delano, California. He invited Dolores to help him start a farm workers' **union** there.

César Chávez had started out as a **migrant** farm worker. He was very quiet and shy, but he was a powerful speaker with good ideas.

18

Dolores and her children moved to Delano, too. Dolores and César decided to call their union The National Farm Workers Association (NFWA). It was still against the law for farm workers to join unions. But it was not against the law for them to join clubs or associations.

This poster shows the NFWA symbol. The black eagle means strength and the white circle stands for hope.

César's wife looked after all the children while César and Dolores drove from town to town, trying to talk workers into joining the union. Both families had to live on a little money that César had saved.

Unions

A union is a kind of club for people who do similar jobs. They join together so they can get better pay and working conditions.

A Rough Start

It was not easy for Dolores and César to talk workers into joining their **union**. Farm workers were afraid they might be fired if growers found out they were organizing. Besides, union **dues** were $3.50 a month. That was about one day's pay for many workers.

Soon, César had used up all of his money. He had to ask people for food to help feed the two families. His wife went back to work in the fields. The children had to take care of each other.

Dolores (to the right of the sign) and other strikers call to those still working and urge them to join the struggle.

When there were about 200 workers in the union, César and Dolores held a big meeting to elect **officers**. Soon, the NFWA started a bank and store for its workers. They helped workers get **life insurance**.

At the first meeting of the NFWA, César (on the right) was elected president and Dolores was elected vice president.

In 1965, the NFWA held an important meeting. They decided to join another workers' association's strike against grape growers. Two groups of workers speaking out against their unfair working conditions might be able to change things.

Strikes

When a union goes on strike, the workers do not go to work. Instead, they walk back and forth outside a factory or business. They carry signs telling everyone that the business is not treating its workers well. Striking workers do not get paid. Their union must have enough money to give them money for food and rent.

Don't Buy Grapes!

The grape **strike** was very difficult. Some growers paid men to beat up the striking workers. Some of them even told the police to arrest workers for things like having a burned out light on a car or stepping onto a grower's field.

The striking farm workers carried signs that said "*Huelga*." This means "strike" in Spanish.

At first the growers were bothered very little by the strike. They brought in workers from Mexico and paid them even less than they paid the striking farm workers. People who ate grapes lived far away from the fields. They did not know about the bad working conditions, so they kept buying grapes.

Dolores and César had to let more people know about the strike. César led a 300-mile (483-kilometer) march from Delano to Sacramento, the capital of California, to **protest** the bad working conditions. Newspapers all over the country carried pictures and stories about the farm workers' problems.

Finally in 1966 a large grape grower called Schenley Industries agreed to treat the farm workers fairly. Dolores wrote the **contract**. The workers would get $1.75 an hour, paid holidays and vacations, and a six-day workweek.

Dolores, César, and the farm workers stood in front of grocery stores. They gave out fliers asking shoppers not to buy grapes.

23

Success and Struggle

After the strike, the NFWA decided to join with another **union**. The new union was called the United Farm Workers' Organizing Committee (UFWOC). Dolores met with more growers. They agreed to sign **contracts** with the UFWOC. The workers knew they could count on Dolores to get them a good deal.

Around this time, Dolores moved to New York to organize **protests** in the East. Soon, people all over the country stopped buying California grapes. By 1970, the UFWOC had contracts with most of California's grape growers.

Dolores married César Chávez's brother Richard (right) when she was in her late 30s. They had four children named Juanita, Maria Elena, Ricky, and Camilla.

Now the UFWOC could work on other problems facing workers. Many of them got sick from poisons that growers made them spray on crops. Dolores met with lawmakers in California and Washington, D.C. She asked them to pass laws making some of the poisons illegal.

Here, César is telling people about poisons that were being sprayed on grapes.

In 1973, the California growers' contracts with the union ran out. Right away, the growers started mistreating the farm workers again. This time, Dolores and César organized a **boycott** of California grapes, lettuce, and wines.

More Troubles

The 1973 **boycott** went on for four years. During that time, Dolores and César began to disagree about how the **union** should be run. Sometimes, Dolores walked out. Other times, César fired her. But Dolores always came back. The two friends could never stop working together for workers' rights.

When **Congress** passed a law allowing farm workers to form unions, the UFWOC changed its name to the United Farm Workers, or UFW.

They started union radio stations so workers could hear union news. They started a medical plan for farm workers. They also started a group that helped workers get good places to live.

When she was beaten up at this protest, Dolores took the police to court. After that, police were not allowed to beat protesters.

In 1978, César called an end to the grape, lettuce, and wine boycott. But in just seven years, growers went back to their old tricks. César called for a new grape boycott. It lasted for almost ten years!

Dolores and César worked night and day to keep people's attention on farm workers' problems. Dolores spent more and more time meeting with lawmakers in California and Washington. She was in her late 50s, but she was still leading **protests**. In 1988, San Francisco police beat up Dolores and other protesters. She was badly hurt.

¡Sí, Se Puede!

When Dolores was 63 years old, César Chávez died. Some growers thought that the **union** would fall apart without César. Some even said that they would not follow the **contracts** they had signed with the union. But Dolores made sure the growers carried out their

President Bill Clinton gave Dolores an award in 1999.

agreements. Today, she is still in charge of making agreements with big companies.

Because of her work, Dolores has received many awards. She is a member of the National Women's Hall of Fame. In 1998 a magazine chose her as a "Woman of the Year."

All of Dolores's eleven children are grown up. Some of them work for the union. She has fourteen grandchildren and four great grandchildren. She loves spending time with them, but she still cares about workers' rights. She is still traveling and meeting with lawmakers.

In her many speeches, she tells people to keep working for change. When she signs autographs she writes, *"Sí, se puede."* "Yes, it can be done."

Dolores is nearly 75 years old. She is still marching and speaking out for workers' and women's rights.

Glossary

activist   person who takes action to make things better for people

boycott   action in which people refuse to buy something

citizen   person who is born in, or moves to a country, and who promises to be loyal to that country in return for certain rights, such as the right to vote

Congress   group of men and women who make laws for the United States

contract   paper that people sign to promise they will do certain things

dues   money a person pays to a club or group they belong to

Latina   Latin-American woman or girl.
A Latin-American man or boy is a Latino.

life insurance   money paid to a person's family if he or she dies

migrant   worker who does not work in one place, but must travel around from job to job

officers   leaders of a group or club, including the president, vice president, secretary, and treasurer

protest   action in which a large group of people speaks out against something that they think is unfair

strike   action in which workers refuse to do their jobs, and walk outside their workplace with signs explaining how the company is being unfair

tavern   place workers go to relax, drink, and eat

union group of workers who join together in order to be paid and treated fairly

World War II war that the United States, Great Britain, the Soviet Union, and France fought against Germany, Japan, and Italy from 1939 to 1945

More Books to Read

An older reader can help you with these books:

Head, Judith. *America's Daughters: 400 Years of American Women.* Los Angeles: Perspective Publishing, 1999.

Perez, Frank. *Dolores Huerta.* Chicago: Raintree, 1995.

Thatcher, Rebecca. *Dolores Huerta.* Hockessin, Delaware: Mitchell Lane Publishers, 2002.

Place to Visit

The Walter P. Reuther Library at Wayne State University

5401 Cass Ave

Detroit MI 48202

313-577-4024

Index

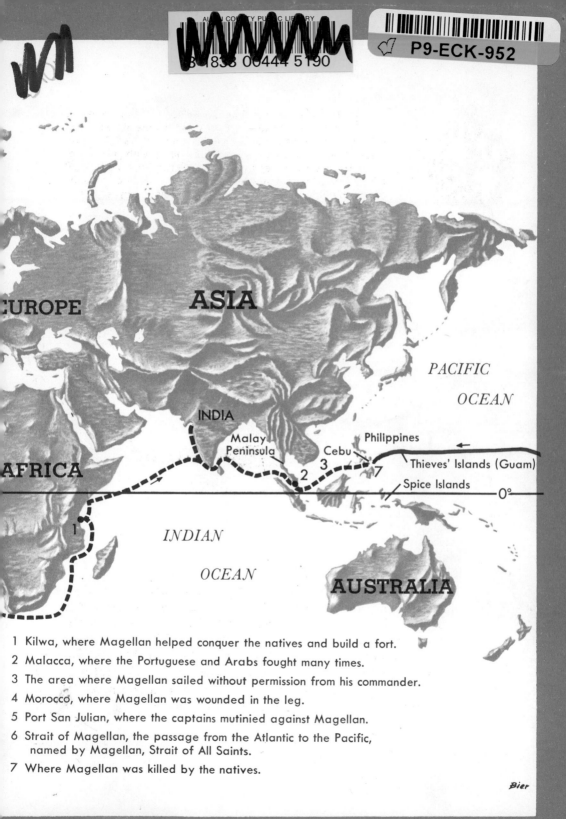

1 Kilwa, where Magellan helped conquer the natives and build a fort.

2 Malacca, where the Portuguese and Arabs fought many times.

3 The area where Magellan sailed without permission from his commander.

4 Morocco, where Magellan was wounded in the leg.

5 Port San Julian, where the captains mutinied against Magellan.

6 Strait of Magellan, the passage from the Atlantic to the Pacific, named by Magellan, Strait of All Saints.

7 Where Magellan was killed by the natives.

THE ASTROLABE, an instrument developed by the Greeks, is the symbol for World Explorer Books. At the time of Columbus, sailors used the astrolabe to chart a ship's course. The arm across the circle could be moved to line up with the sun or a star. Using the number indicated by the pointer, a sailor could tell his approximate location on the sea. Although the astrolabe was not completely accurate, it helped many early explorers in their efforts to conquer the unknown.

World Explorer Books are written especially for children who love adventure and exploration into the unknown. Designed for young readers, each book has been tested by the Dale-Chall readability formula. Leo Fay, Ph.D., Professor of Education at Indiana University, is educational consultant for the series. Dr. Fay, an experienced teacher and lecturer, is well known for his professional bulletins and text material in both elementary reading and social studies.

A WORLD EXPLORER

Ferdinand Magellan

BY LYNN GROH

ILLUSTRATED BY ROBERT DOREMUS

GARRARD PUBLISHING COMPANY
CHAMPAIGN, ILLINOIS

For George's Girls

This series is edited by Elizabeth Minot Graves

1614705

Contents

1

In the Queen's Palace

"Come on, Ferdinand! We can't watch the ships all day," Francisco Serrano shouted to his cousin. The harbor of Lisbon was very busy. He had to shout to be heard.

Ferdinand Magellan wished that he *could* watch the ships all day. But he knew he had to return to the palace.

"I'll race you to the end of the pier!" he called to Francisco.

The boys ran in and out among the busy workers. Ferdinand was smaller than Francisco, but he was quicker. He moved his short legs as fast as he could.

"I won! I beat you!" he cried.

It was always important to Ferdinand to win. Maybe that was because he was smaller than other twelve-year-old boys. He had to prove that he was not a weakling.

When the two boys reached the great palace, they became very quiet. They stood straight and marched in step.

"Did I get dirt on my uniform?"

"You look all right," Francisco said in a whisper.

Ferdinand and Francisco lived at the palace. They were pages to the Queen of Portugal. There were many other pages at the palace. All of them were the sons of noblemen. When they grew up they would be leaders in the army or the navy. But first they had to learn many things. The palace was their school.

Their classes began each day after breakfast. The boys studied map-making. They learned to find directions from the stars. They studied arithmetic and Latin.

When the schoolwork was finished, they went into the palace courtyard. There they learned how to fight with swords. At first Ferdinand needed to use both hands to lift the heavy sword. He also learned to fight on horseback with a lance, or long spear.

Ferdinand's older brother, Diogo, was a page too. Diogo tried to help Ferdinand. But Ferdinand wanted to do everything by himself.

Sometimes Ferdinand felt homesick for

his mother and father and his sister, Isabel. But there was little time to be homesick at the busy palace.

Ferdinand had many duties. He ran errands for the Queen. Sometimes he went to the big hall, where the King and Queen received visitors. There he called out the names of visitors as they entered.

Later, Ferdinand waited on tables in the huge dining hall. Important visitors often stayed for meals. Some were rich princes. Some were army officers, in colorful uniforms. Others were brave sea captains who had been to faraway lands.

One evening the guests were excitedly talking about a daring explorer, who had just returned from a long voyage.

"Imagine! A whole new world!" the King said.

"By sailing westward!"

"There must be great riches there!"

Ferdinand hurried to find Francisco. "Who are they talking about? What has happened?" Ferdinand asked excitedly.

"Christopher Columbus," Francisco said. "He found a new land on the other side of the world!"

"Do you think we might go there some day?" Ferdinand asked. His eyes shone.

"Maybe. But Columbus did it *first*. He is a famous man," Francisco said.

Ferdinand Magellan sat quietly for a moment. Then he said, "Someday I will be a famous man!"

2

Holiday at Home

Ferdinand and Diogo rode up the hill to their big, stone castle. They sat very straight on their horses, like soldiers. They were going home to visit their mother and father.

The castle was really an old fort. The family lived on the top floor. The farm animals were kept on the ground floor. There they could be protected against wild animals. Many nobles used their castles in that way.

Ferdinand's mother, Dona Alda, ran out to the courtyard. She threw her arms around the boys and kissed them. When she looked at Ferdinand, she said, "Oh, how my little boy has grown!"

Dom Ruy came out. "This is no little boy!" he shouted. "He is almost a man! He is fourteen years old."

He gave Ferdinand a mighty slap on the shoulder, the way knights greeted each other at the palace. "We will go boar hunting together," Dom Ruy cried. "I will see how well my sons have learned to shoot."

Early the next morning, Dom Ruy and his sons got their crossbows ready. They rode their horses past the farm workers picking grapes. Soon they were deep in the forest.

The hunting dogs began to bark. They

had found a herd of wild boars. Ferdinand dashed ahead. When the boars saw him, they snorted fiercely. They bared their long, sharp tusks. They pawed the ground with their hooves.

Ferdinand took a deep breath. He aimed carefully with his crossbow. He shot at the biggest boar in the group. The animal fell dead! The others ran away.

Dom Ruy galloped up. "Well done!" he shouted proudly.

"We will have roast boar tomorrow," Diogo said. "A holiday feast!"

"You will not have many more holidays together," Dom Ruy said, as they rode home. "Soon Diogo will be ready to go to sea."

"I am ready to go now!" Ferdinand said.

Dom Ruy and Diogo laughed.

"Later, Ferdinand," his father said. "In a few years you will be old enough."

"One day I will be a captain," Ferdinand said. "I will sail west and find new lands, just like Columbus. I will be famous!"

"You will be the shortest famous man in history!" Diogo teased him.

"Never mind, Ferdinand," Dom Ruy said. "Even little men can do big things."

3

Sailor Without a Ship

Ferdinand sat at a long, wooden table. He was copying a list into a big book. It was a romantic list: figs, biscuits, wines, baking ovens, "looking glasses," fish hooks. These were among the supplies that ships carried on a voyage to strange lands.

But Ferdinand did not feel romantic. He had not been chosen to make the voyage!

Other men sat writing at long tables too. They were clerks, like Ferdinand and Francisco. They kept records and did other chores.

The place where they worked was called India House. It was the great supply center for ships going to the Orient.

There was much excitement there now. Messengers rushed in and out. Captains and commanders came in to give orders.

In only two more days, a great fleet would sail for India. The ships would bring back spices, such as cinnamon and pepper. The people of Europe would pay much gold for the spices. The crews of the ships would get a share of the gold. They would be rich!

How Ferdinand wished that he could go! He was twenty years old, and was considered a man. Many men who had served as pages with him in the royal court had gone to sea years before. But there was a new King ruling Portugal, and Ferdinand's family was not in this King's favor. So Ferdinand was still a lowly clerk.

"Dom Magellan!" a voice spoke sharply.

Ferdinand stood. His head came only to the shoulder of the young officer who stood beside him. Ferdinand was still very short.

"Some of our supplies are missing," the officer said. "We should have ten more barrels of salt beef. And we have no raisins at all!"

"I'll see to it, sir," Ferdinand said, bowing.

Ferdinand turned and left the room.

Francisco caught up with him outside the door. "I'm going with you," he said.

"There is too much ink and not enough action back there!"

The cousins walked along the bustling waterfront until they reached a great warehouse, where barrels of food were waiting to be put on the ships.

"One of my ships is short ten barrels of beef," Ferdinand said to the foreman.

"No, you are not short, Dom Magellan," the foreman replied. "Everything is here. But it takes time to load ships for a year's voyage."

It was turning dark now. "Let's hurry home," Francisco said. "We must get ready for the big celebration tonight. We are all invited, you know! There will be dancing, and lots to eat!"

"I will be along later," Ferdinand said. "I am going to call on Dom John first."

"John of Lisbon? That strange old

man!" Francisco said. "He never talks of anything but maps and mathematics. I can't understand most of it."

"Vasco da Gama found the way to India with maps and mathematics," Ferdinand said. "There must be other lands to find!"

John of Lisbon greeted Ferdinand warmly. He was a famous man. It was said that he knew more about sailing than anyone else in Europe. He had been Ferdinand's teacher. Now they were good friends.

"Is your fleet ready to sail, Ferdinand?" Dom John teased.

"*My* fleet!" Ferdinand said unhappily. "I am a sailor without a ship. Do you think I will be a clerk all my life?"

"Your turn will come, Ferdinand," Dom John assured him. "There will be many voyages to the Orient, now that we know the way. Portugal will become rich in the spice trade."

"I don't want to be rich," Ferdinand said. "I want to explore the world."

"Maybe you will do that, too," Dom John replied. He thought for a moment, then went on. "Columbus thought that he would find the Orient by sailing west. He did not find it. Vasco da Gama sailed east, and found it. But I still think Columbus was right. I believe there is a westward way. Maybe you will find it some day, Ferdinand!"

"Some day!" Ferdinand said. "What will I do while I wait for 'some day?'"

"Learn, my son!" said John of Lisbon. "Learn about maps, and the stars, and currents. Learn about ships, and how to sail them. You can never learn *too much*!"

4

To Sea at Last!

The harbor of Lisbon was white with sails. Twenty ships were putting out to sea. They carried 2,000 soldiers.

Ferdinand and his cousin, Francisco, waved happily from their ship. They were strong young men now, twenty-three years old. They were off to sea at last!

"Tie your trunks tight to the deck," a sailor shouted.

Ferdinand and Francisco tied their small sea chests to the deck. They tied a suit of armor to each chest. Finally, they tied a bedroll on top of the pile.

The ship was very small. Only the top officers had cabins. Everyone else lived on the open deck. It was very crowded.

"I think I will tie *me* to the deck," Ferdinand laughed. "The trip around Africa is stormy, they say."

Ferdinand was thrilled about the adventure ahead of them. The fleet would sail all the way around Africa, then on to India. Several fleets had sailed to India before. But this was the biggest fleet of all. The Portuguese were going to build forts in India. They had to protect their rich spice trade from enemy merchants.

The ships sailed south for many weeks. At first it was very hot. Then they reached the cold Antarctic seas. Great waves swept over the decks of the ships. Ferdinand's wet clothes froze. They rubbed on his body and made painful sores.

One day there was a dreadful storm. Waves dashed and dashed against the little ship that Ferdinand was on. Boards broke. Water poured in. Another big wave hit the ship. It began to sink!

"Abandon ship!" the Captain shouted.

The crew lowered the longboats. There were not enough boats for everyone. Ferdinand and some other men jumped into the icy water. They held on to the sides of the longboats. Finally, they were rescued by other ships in the fleet.

"Do you still want to find new lands?" Francisco asked.

"Yes!" Ferdinand said. His teeth were chattering. "But next time, I will have a stronger ship!"

Finally they came to an African town called Kilwa. The Portuguese wanted to

stop there to get fresh food and water. But the African chief would not let them land.

The Portuguese commander was angry. "We will fight them," he said. "We will conquer this chief!"

Ferdinand was in one of the first long-boats that rowed ashore. He saw the native warriors waiting on the beach. The warriors waved long spears. They held

up shields made of animal skins. They
had painted their faces so they would
look very fierce.

The warriors rushed toward the boats,
shouting wildly. Ferdinand took tight hold
of his sword. He jumped out of his longboat. He ran up on the beach to do his
part in the battle.

Boom! Boom! Cannons fired from the
ships in the harbor. Some of the natives

ran away. They had never heard such a fearful noise before. But many natives fought bravely. Ferdinand fought bravely too. Finally the natives gave up.

When the battle ended, the Portuguese commander sent for Ferdinand.

"We are going to build a fort here," the commander told Ferdinand. "We will need men like you. I want you to stay here and help me defend the fort."

5

In the Spice Lands

Ferdinand stood at the prow of his ship. He looked eagerly across the water. A strange new land lay there before him.

Ferdinand had spent two years in Africa. His job had been important. But he had longed to sail on. Now, at last, he had reached India.

The Portuguese and Arabs were fighting a war in India. They were fighting over the spice trade. The Arabs wanted to keep this rich trade for themselves. They were trying to drive the Portuguese out of India.

Soon Ferdinand was fighting in some of these battles. Many of the greatest battles were at sea.

Once an Arab boat rammed Ferdinand's ship. The Arabs leaped onto the deck, waving their big curved swords. They rushed at the Portuguese. Ferdinand saw his Captain struck down!

Ferdinand hurried to help his Captain. He stood over him, swinging his sword to keep the Arabs away. But the Arabs attacked from every side. Ferdinand was stabbed. Then he was wounded again! He kept fighting as long as he could. But he finally fell. Blood was pouring from his cuts.

At last the Arabs were beaten. But Ferdinand's Captain was dead. Ferdinand was almost dead, too. His friends found him, lying on top of the Captain he had

tried to save. It was six months before he was well.

Ferdinand's next great adventure was at Malacca. This was a rich trading center in the Malay Peninsula, southeast of India. The ruler there seemed friendly.

Ferdinand and his cousin, Francisco, went together to visit the famous markets. They saw shops filled with spices, silk, sparkling jewels and beautiful pieces of carved ivory.

But something was wrong. The cousins could tell from the strange way the people looked at them. They heard the natives whispering. Francisco pretended not to hear, but he listened closely. He understood the native language.

"These people do not like us," he told Ferdinand. "I think they are planning to attack us! You hurry back and warn

34

the Admiral. I will stay here and try to learn more. They don't suspect that I know what they are saying."

The cousins then agreed on a plan. Ferdinand would watch from the ship. If there were danger, Francisco would signal from the pier.

The Admiral laughed at Ferdinand's warning. The Arabs acted friendly. Many of them came and held parties on the ships. But Ferdinand kept watch anyway. Finally he saw Francisco on the pier. Francisco gave the danger signal!

The Portuguese sprang upon the Arabs who were visiting the ships. The Arabs were armed! They had planned to take the Portuguese by surprise.

More Arab soldiers swarmed about the ships in small boats. The Portuguese fired their cannons. They beat off the Arabs.

But Francisco and several companions were trapped on the pier.

"We can't leave Francisco!" Ferdinand cried.

Ferdinand leaped into a longboat and started rowing ashore. Arab spears fell all around him as he raced through the water. But Ferdinand was lucky. He made it to the pier and rescued Francisco.

"Ferdinand, you are a true friend," Francisco said. "But you are too daring. Someday you will be killed trying to help someone else."

The Portuguese went back to India. Months later they returned to Malacca with a large army. This time, Ferdinand was a captain. He led his men in a wild charge through the city streets.

The Arabs fought fiercely. Many rode on war elephants. The great animals

swung their trunks like giant clubs. The Portuguese fired their crossbows. The elephants trumpeted in fear and ran away. The Portuguese captured the city.

Afterwards Francisco was sent to the Spice Islands, to the east. He and Ferdinand hugged each other when they parted. They did not know they would never see each other again.

Ferdinand stayed at Malacca a year and a half. While there, he bought a slave named Enrique. Enrique told him that he had heard of some islands beyond the Spice Islands. Ferdinand longed to explore them. But the Portuguese admiral would not let him go.

One day, Ferdinand did a foolish thing. He sailed away without permission! He took Enrique with him as one of the crew.

Ferdinand sailed east for about two thousand miles. He found islands no white man had ever seen before. The natives spoke a language of their own, but some of them spoke Malay too. That was Enrique's language! The natives told Enrique that there were hundreds of tiny islands with many spices.

Ferdinand was very excited. He did not have enough ships or supplies to explore the islands. He hurried back to Malacca. Ferdinand hoped the Admiral would send a fleet to the new islands.

But the Admiral was very angry. "We don't need any more islands! We have enough spices to make all of us rich!" he shouted. "We cannot use men who disobey orders. You must go back to Portugal!"

6

A King's Anger

Now Ferdinand Magellan went home in disgrace.

The King would not let him come to the palace. Old friends would have nothing to do with him.

One friend was loyal to Ferdinand. That was John of Lisbon.

"You are a good soldier, Magellan," John said. "But you must learn to obey your commanders."

Ferdinand knew that John was right. But now he had no commanders to obey.

John helped Ferdinand get another chance. This time Ferdinand was sent to Morocco, in North Africa. The Portuguese had captured Morocco, but the natives there were rebelling.

Ferdinand fought for several months in Morocco. Once he led soldiers in a fierce attack against a walled city. They had to climb the walls while the enemy threw spears down on them.

Ferdinand tried to pull himself over the wall. A native reached for him with a sword. Ferdinand dodged, but not in time. His leg was badly cut. Because of that wound, Ferdinand walked with a limp for the rest of his life.

Ferdinand won many honors in Morocco. But he could not get along with the other officers. They quarreled. He was sent home again.

Now the King became very angry with Ferdinand. He thought that Ferdinand was a troublemaker.

John of Lisbon was still Ferdinand's friend. He knew that Ferdinand often got into trouble because he wanted to do daring things.

"Why don't you do something big?" John said to Ferdinand. "Why don't you try to sail around the world? You have dreamed of it for years."

Most people thought it was impossible to sail around the world. They said the New World was solid land, dividing the world's great oceans. There was no way for ships to get through, they said.

John of Lisbon did not agree. He felt that there was a water passage through the New World. He thought it might be a shorter way to the Spice Islands.

"Others have looked for the passage," he told Ferdinand. "But they stopped too soon. You must look farther south."

"King Manuel probably would not send me on such a voyage," Ferdinand said unhappily. "But I will ask him anyway."

The King was still angry. He would not even talk to Ferdinand.

Ferdinand made a plan. There was a special day at the palace, when beggars could see the King. The King sat on a throne in a big room. The beggars came before him and bowed. They asked for money and favors. Ferdinand joined them.

All around Ferdinand were men in rags. A nobleman did not belong with such beggars. But Ferdinand stood there straight and proud.

When his turn came, Ferdinand bowed to the King. He said, "Your Majesty, I

would like ships and men for a voyage around the world!"

The King was too angry to speak for a moment. Then he began to shout cruel things at Ferdinand.

"You are not a nobleman, Magellan. You are a beggar! I have no need for the services of a beggar."

There was no longer a place for Ferdinand in his own country. Sadly, he left Portugal forever. He went over the mountains to Spain.

One day King Manuel would be sorry that he had driven Ferdinand away.

7

Under a New Flag

Once again, Ferdinand Magellan stood before a king. This time, it was King Charles of Spain.

Ferdinand told King Charles about his plan to find the westward passage and to sail around the world.

"I have heard some explorers say there might be a passage," King Charles said. "But it is a dangerous voyage. They have all turned back."

"I will not turn back!" Ferdinand said. "I will sail until I find the passage!"

King Charles looked at this bold soldier from Portugal. Ferdinand was a short man. He walked with a limp. But he was not a weakling. His face was lined by the hard life he had lived, fighting for his own country. He had scars from many battle wounds.

"I believe you," King Charles said. "You look like a man who would not turn back. I will give you ships and men to sail around the world! You will share the riches if you find a new way to the Spice Islands."

Magellan was given five ships. They were very old and they leaked. It took almost two years to get them ready for the trip.

This was a happy time for Magellan. He married a very beautiful girl named Beatriz Barbosa. A year later, a son was born to them. They named him Rodrigo.

At last, the five ships were ready. Food for the voyage was put in barrels and stored aboard the ships.

Magellan would lead the way in the *Trinidad*. Each of the other four ships had a captain. The *San Antonio* was the largest, and carried the most supplies. The smallest was the little *Santiago*. The other two ships were named *Victoria* and *Concepcion*.

Ferdinand said good-by to Beatriz and little Rodrigo. The ships sailed out of the harbor of Seville, Spain.

Ferdinand was hardly at sea when he found that he had been cheated. Some of the barrels which had been put on the ships were not filled with food. They were filled with sawdust! There was not enough food for the trip. His men would

have starved! Some enemy did not want them to make the voyage.

The enemy was King Manuel from Portugal. His spies had learned about Ferdinand's voyage. King Manuel was afraid that Spain would find a short way to the Spice Islands. He had told his spies to put sawdust in the food barrels.

Angrily, Ferdinand turned back to get more food. This time, he looked in each barrel before it was put on a ship. He made sure that every barrel was full of food.

On September 20, 1519, the ships sailed again. This time, they did not turn back.

8

The Great Voyage Begins

A winter storm beat against the five ships. The wind howled. The waves grew larger and larger. Water broke over the decks.

The wind grew even worse. It tipped the ships further and further. At any moment, they might tip over.

"Lower the sails!" Magellan ordered. The men crept over the icy deck. They held the rigging tightly as they worked. If they let go, they might be swept overboard.

At last the storm was over. But there were many others. The men wished they had never left Spain.

Three hard months passed before the lookout finally shouted: "Land ho!"

Magellan rushed to the rail. There was land at last! He had reached South America. He sailed down the coast and stopped in a quiet bay. Today, there is a big city there called Rio de Janeiro.

That night, Magellan saw fires burning at the edge of a forest. Next morning, some Indians came out of the forest to look at the ships.

Magellan and his men rowed ashore, carrying weapons. But the Indians were friendly. They wore few clothes. Their faces were painted.

Magellan made signs to tell the Indians he wanted food. They brought fresh fruit

and meat. Magellan paid for the food
with bells and other trinkets from Spain.

The Indians liked the little bells best
of all. They had never seen bells before.
They tied them on their arms and legs.
Then they danced, and the bells tinkled.
The Indians laughed gaily.

The sailors were happy there. But soon
Magellan said, "Weigh anchor! We must
find the passage!"

The five ships sailed south. Magellan
watched the shore carefully. He explored
many bays and inlets. But he could not
find a passage. The men grew more and
more discouraged.

And now the Antarctic winter began.
Again there were terrible storms. The
rain turned to sleet and snow. The sails
froze.

The men became stiff with cold. Waves

washed over the decks and soaked them to the skin. Their wet clothing froze. Their ears and toes were frostbitten. The men could hardly move to do their work.

The high wind made it too dangerous to light fires. The men had to eat raw salt meat, or soggy biscuits and raisins. They could have no lights at night. They had to work in the dark!

Magellan stayed up on deck day and night. He helped the men do their work. He took care of the sick and injured. He ate what the sailors ate. When he did go to his cabin, it was only for a short nap. He did not even take off his wet clothes!

The men were proud of their leader. For two months they stood by him and bravely fought the storms. But then they became too tired to go on. The men begged to return home to their families.

Magellan would not turn back. He looked for a place to rest. On March 31, 1520, he found another great bay. He named it Port San Julian.

"We can go no farther in these storms," Magellan said. "We will spend the winter here."

9

Mutiny!

The men went ashore to explore. It felt good to walk on the ground again, after months on the ships.

The land was a dreadful disappointment. It was frozen and empty. The sailors shivered as they looked for food and fresh water. They found water. But they could find no food of any kind, not even berries or roots. There were no trees. The men cut dwarfed bushes for firewood.

"There is no life here," they told Magellan. "We will die if we stay here. We want to go home."

"This is the end of the world!"

"The world has no end," Magellan said. "It is round, and we will find the way to sail around it."

"What will we eat?" the men argued. "Our supplies will not last long, and there is no food here."

"There are many fish in the bay," Magellan said. "We will eat fish. We will save the food we have. From now on, we will have bread and wine only once a day."

At this the men grumbled still more. Even the ships' captains turned against Magellan. They had wanted to turn back many times. Now they went to Magellan again.

"We have searched for months," they said. "There is no passage! Our men are tired and hungry. We must go home. The King would not expect us to stay here and die."

"The King ordered me to find the passage," Magellan said. "And he ordered you to obey me. We shall not turn back."

The captains continued to grumble among themselves.

"We do not have to obey him," said Captain Quesada, of the *Concepcion*. "We are four, and he is only one. We can return to Spain without him!"

Captain John Serrano of the *Santiago* was angry when he heard such talk. "That is mutiny!" he cried. "I have sworn an oath to be loyal. I am for the King and Magellan!"

"And I am with you!" joined in

Captain Mesquita of the *San Antonio*.

"Well, I am for the King and myself!" said Captain Quesada. "I say we should turn back."

Captain Mendoza of the *Victoria* agreed with him. "We have to do something to stop this mad man, or we will never see Spain again!"

Mesquita and Serrano argued with them. "We cannot mutiny!" they said. "Wait. We will talk to Magellan again. Maybe he will change his mind."

The two unfriendly captains pretended to agree. But that night they decided to act. Captain Quesada and his men crept aboard the *San Antonio*. They put the loyal Captain Mesquita in irons. They took over his ship!

Now there were three ships against only two! The wicked captains had the

San Antonio, Victoria and *Concepcion.* These were the biggest ships, with the most men and cannon. Magellan had only his *Trinidad* and the tiny *Santiago,* led by loyal Captain Serrano.

The rebels were sure they had won. They sent a message to Magellan. "If you will agree to return to Spain, we will make you the commander again. If you do not, we will sink your ships. We will tell the King you were wrecked in a storm!"

Magellan would not give up easily. But he could not fight three ships. Carefully he made a plan. He wrote a note to Captain Mendoza. The note said that the captains must give up or they would be killed. Magellan picked a few of his bravest men to deliver the note.

These sailors rowed to the *Victoria.*

They acted friendly, but had weapons hidden in their clothes. One of the sailors took the note to Mendoza. The wicked captain laughed when he read the note. While he laughed, one of the brave men quickly pulled out a knife. He stabbed Captain Mendoza!

Now all of Magellan's men attacked. The plotters were surprised. After a short battle, the men of the *Victoria* gave up.

Magellan had three ships now. He did not want to sink the other two. He needed them. He also thought of the men on those ships, who had sailed so long. What could he do?

Then a lucky thing happened. A storm arose. The winds blew hard against the *San Antonio*. The ship's anchor did not hold. The ship was pushed toward the rocks!

The men of the *San Antonio* were too busy to fight. They were trying to put up sails, to keep the ship off the rocks. Magellan ordered his cannons fired. Then his loyal men swarmed over the side of the *San Antonio*. Captain Quesada was forced to surrender.

A disloyal officer named Cartagena had taken command of the *Concepcion*. When he saw that he stood alone, Cartagena gave up too.

Magellan held a trial. Captain Mendoza was already dead. The other two wicked captains were found guilty of mutiny. They had rebelled against their leader. This was a very serious crime.

Captain Quesada was beheaded. The men had to watch so they would know what happened to a captain when he was disloyal.

Cartagena was put in irons. He was a special favorite of the King. "I will spare your life," Magellan told Cartagena. "But you are not fit to serve with my fleet. When we sail on, I will leave you here!"

Forty sailors who had helped the wicked captains were also sentenced to die. But then Magellan pardoned them. He put them in chains, and put them to work at hard labor.

The men did not dare to rebel again. They feared the terrible winter in this unknown land. But they feared their stern commander even more.

10

Land of the "Big Feet"

Magellan's men worked at repairing the ships. They fixed broken masts and mended sails. They made new clothes for themselves.

A scouting party went out in longboats. The men were to look for food in other parts of the bay. They returned with some strange creatures, which they called "sea wolves" and "sea geese." Actually, they were seals and penguins. Magellan's men had a feast of fresh meat!

Two months passed. The men were cold and homesick. They longed to see their families.

They had seen no people here. They thought the land was deserted. But one day a giant came near on shore! He was the tallest man they had ever seen. His clothes were made of animal skins. He had very big feet. He wore fur shoes that made his feet seem even bigger.

The giant danced and sang in a strange, high voice. While he danced, he poured sand over his head! Magellan sent a man ashore. The sailor danced and sang too, and poured sand over his head. The giant was very shy, but slowly he came closer. Finally, he agreed to go aboard the *Trinidad*.

Later, the giant brought other members of his tribe. They wanted to see the ships. They laughed at the short white men. Magellan called them "Patagonians," which means "big feet." That is still their name today.

Weeks passed, and the winter continued. Magellan sent the *Santiago* on a scouting trip. The men were to look for food. They were also to look for the passage. Magellan thought it might be near.

The *Santiago* sailed about sixty miles. The men sighted an inlet! They sailed into it. But it proved to be a river. They named it the Santa Cruz.

The *Santiago* sailed back into the bay. The lookout saw hundreds of seals and penguins on a beach. The captain sent men ashore to capture them for food.

Suddenly a storm arose. The men could not get back to the ship. The storm dashed the little *Santiago* on to the shore.

The ship broke into pieces! The men were saved, but all of their supplies were lost.

Now there was even less food. The men of the *Santiago* had to walk back to the fleet. They were divided among the four ships that were left.

Magellan moved his fleet to the mouth of the Santa Cruz River. He sent men ashore to kill seals. The seal meat was smoked, then packed in salt. But soon all of the salt was gone. Without salt, the meat would spoil.

"We can wait no longer for spring weather," Magellan said. "We will starve if we stay here. It is better to face the storms."

Once more, the ships sailed south.

11

The Passage!

Two months passed. The winter storms continued. The men were cold and hungry. Many were sick.

On October 21, 1520, the lookout saw another inlet. It looked frightening. The water was black. High, bare mountains rose on both sides. There were no trees. There was no sign of life of any kind.

"There can be only evil demons in such a place!" the men cried.

"We shall see!" Magellan said.

The four ships sailed into the inlet. Suddenly, a storm began! It was worse than any they had seen before. Wild winds blew. The sky grew as dark as night. Magellan's *Trinidad* was almost dashed upon the rocks.

When the storm ended, Magellan could see only the *Victoria*. The two other ships were nowhere in sight! Could they have sunk in the storm?

Two days, three days passed. Fearfully, Magellan kept watch. He thought he would never see his comrades again.

But on the fourth day, the lookout saw a sail. "Sail ho!" he shouted joyfully. The ships were safe!

The ships came closer. Magellan could see the men, dancing wildly on the decks. Finally he could hear shouts from the

San Antonio. "We have found it! We have found the passage!"

It had been a lucky storm. Instead of wrecking the ships, it had blown them right into the passage. The search was over!

Surely Magellan would go home now, the men thought. They had been sailing for a whole year. They had made a great discovery. Someone else could come later and explore the new ocean.

"No!" Magellan said. "We must go on! We will be the first to sail around the world!"

But the captain of the *San Antonio* did not want to go on. Secretly, he told his crew, "Magellan knows nothing about this new ocean. We might be lost forever. Let us go home without him."

The crew agreed. One night the *San*

Antonio slipped off and sailed for Spain.

Now Magellan had only three ships. Still he sailed on through the passage. He explored all the inlets. He made maps, so that people who came later could find their way.

Magellan named the passage the Straits of All Saints. Later the name was changed to Straits of Magellan, in honor of the man who found it.

One day the three ships sailed into a broad bay. Beyond the bay was the ocean!

The men went wild with joy. They laughed. They cried. They fell to their knees on the decks to pray. Magellan was so happy that the tears ran down his cheeks.

"This new ocean is so peaceful," he said, remembering the fierce storms on the Atlantic. "We will call it 'Pacific.'"

12

Starvation

"Water! Water!" a man cried weakly from the deck of the *Trinidad*.

Magellan knelt beside the sick man. He tried to comfort him. But there was nothing Magellan could do. There was no water.

There was no food, either. Men were lying all about on the deck. Many of them were too weak to move. Nineteen of them had already died. They were starving.

They had sailed the Pacific for three months without finding land. The food and water barrels had been empty for weeks.

The men had water only when it rained. They ate rats caught on the ships. They chewed sawdust. They had even torn the leather off the ships' masts and tried to eat that. They dragged the leather in the ocean until it was soft. Then they cooked it over open fires.

The sick men were almost mad from hunger. Many thought they saw land when there was no land. One day, a weak voice called out, "Land ho!" The men paid no attention. They had heard that call too often. They did not believe it.

But Magellan hurried to the front of the ship. "We are saved!" he shouted to his crew. "There are islands!"

Men who were strong enough went to the rail. They wept when they saw land, green and cool, before them. Then they saw many little boats put out from one of the islands. The boats had sails made of palm leaves. The natives in the boats were small and brown skinned men. They wore no clothes at all.

The natives climbed all over the three big ships. They were very friendly. They laughed and talked to each other. But they stole everything they could find. They picked up clothes, suits of armor, and rope. They even took swords from the men. Then they stole one of the longboats. Magellan's men were too weak to stop them.

Magellan picked the strongest men in the crews. He sent them ashore to get food and water. They were also to bring

back all the things the natives had stolen.

Forty men went ashore. They were so angry at the natives that they burned the little village.

The natives did not seem to mind. Their huts were made of grass. They could build new ones easily.

They were still friendly. They gave the men all the food they could eat. Magellan paid for the food with trinkets. But he could not forget that the natives were really thieves. "We will call these islands Ladrones, the Thieves' Islands," he said.

The men rested, and grew strong again. They sailed on.

Soon the explorers reached some very large islands. Magellan thought that they were the Spice Islands at last. This was not so. He had discovered the Philippines!

13

A Famous Man

Magellan stopped at Cebu, one of the Philippine Islands. When he anchored in the harbor, a boat came out from shore. The boat was covered with flowers. In the middle sat a man dressed in bright robes.

The chief, or Rajah, of Cebu had come to meet Magellan!

Magellan had brought his Malaccan slave, Enrique, on the voyage. The Rajah understood Enrique's Malay language.

With Enrique's help, Magellan and the Rajah talked to each other.

"Did you come from India or China?" the Rajah asked.

"No, we came from the other side of the world!" Magellan said. "But how do you know about India and China? Are they near here?"

"Oh, yes," the Rajah replied. "Ships often come here from those rich lands."

Magellan asked some more questions about the islands. Then he almost shouted for joy. These were the same islands he had found before, when he sailed from India without permission! He had proved that ships can sail all around the world!

"We will rest here a few days," Magellan said to his men. "Then we will sail to the Spice Islands. From there we will go to India and Africa, then home to Spain. We will be the first to circle the world!"

The Rajah sent for the chiefs of the other islands. He asked them to meet this great captain from a faraway land.

The chiefs came, with many of their people. They asked Magellan questions about the people of Europe. They asked about the white man's God. Many of them became Christians.

But one chief did not like Magellan. His name was Silapulapu.

Silapulapu told the other chiefs, "Have nothing to do with these foreign devils! You must not worship their God. You will make our own gods angry. Send these people away!"

"We must teach Silapulapu a lesson," Magellan said to his men. "We will capture his island!"

"No, no!" the Rajah said. "Silapulapu is powerful. He has many warriors. You might be killed!"

Magellan's men were also against the plan. "We do not want to fight," they said. "We still have a long voyage before us. We want to go home."

Magellan would not listen. He chose some of his best men. They rowed to the island where Silapulapu ruled.

There were many rocks around the island. The boats could not land. Magellan told some of his men to wait in the boats. Then he called to the others to follow him. He jumped into the water and began wading ashore.

But Silapulapu had been warned! His warriors were waiting. There were many hundreds of warriors. Magellan had only forty men.

The warriors ran to attack Magellan. They threw spears. Some shot poisoned arrows! At first the spears and arrows bounced off the thick armor which Magellan's men wore. But the natives were clever. They aimed at the legs, which were not covered by armor. When Magellan's men fell, the warriors rushed in to stab them and club them.

The men who had stayed in the boats tried to help. They shot their crossbows. But the boats were too far away. The arrows fell into the water.

Magellan saw that the battle was lost. "Go back!" he shouted to his brave men. "Back to the boats!"

The men ran toward the boats. But Magellan stayed behind. He was trying to help the wounded. Now many warriors attacked Magellan.

Magellan was wounded in the leg with
a spear. He could hardly stand. Another
spear hit his arm. His helmet was knocked
off. He fought back, killing a warrior
with his lance. Then his lance fell. He
tried to draw his sword. But he could not
move his injured arm. He was helpless!

Magellan started to wade toward the
boats. But the warriors were all around
him. They knocked him into the water.

They stabbed him again and again.

Magellan's men watched helplessly from the boats. They could do nothing. They saw their brave leader fall and die. Many of them wept.

"He could have made it to the boats," they said. "But he stayed to help the wounded. He died trying to save them."

The men who were left went on to the Spice Islands. But they were still far from home. They had to face many new dangers. And now they were without their strong leader to guide them.

Only one ship finished the long voyage around Africa and back to Spain. Only eighteen men were left of the 265 who had started out three years before.

The eighteen men went to church together as soon as they got off their ship. They wanted to give thanks for their good fortune. Then there was a great celebration. The sailors paraded through the streets. They were heroes.

Magellan did not live to see the glad celebration. But he had led the great voyage. He had shown the way. His name became known everywhere as that of a daring world explorer.

Ferdinand Magellan did become a famous man!

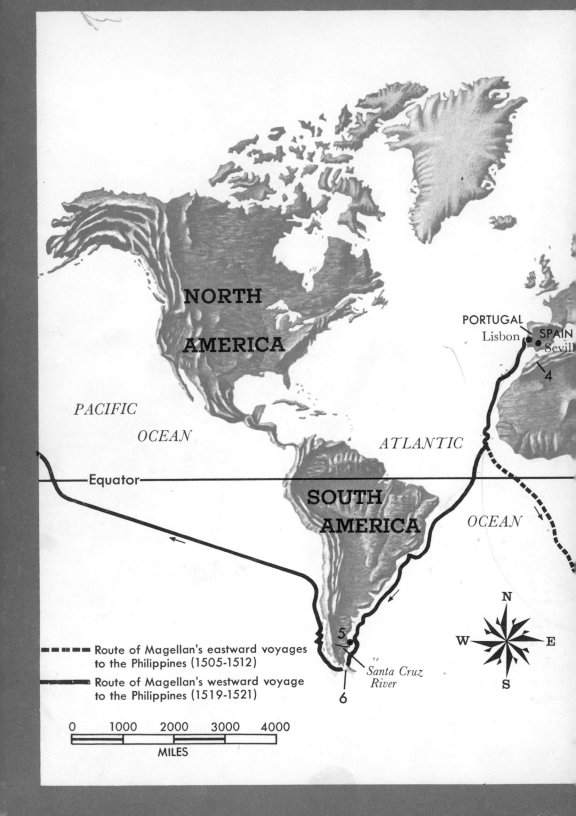

NORTH

AMERICA

PACIFIC

OCEAN

PORTUGAL SPAIN
Lisbon Sevill

4

ATLANTIC

Equator

SOUTH

AMERICA OCEAN

5

Santa Cruz
River

6

━ ━ ━ ━ ━ Route of Magellan's eastward voyages
to the Philippines (1505-1512)

━━━━━ Route of Magellan's westward voyage
to the Philippines (1519-1521)

N

W E

S

0   1000   2000   3000   4000
MILES